BRITAIN'S
BENDY BUSES

KEITH A. JENKINSON

AMBERLEY

First published 2019

Amberley Publishing
The Hill, Stroud
Gloucestershire, GL5 4EP

www.amberley-books.com

Copyright © Keith A. Jenkinson, 2019

The right of Keith A. Jenkinson to be identified
as the Author of this work has been asserted
in accordance with the Copyright, Designs and
Patents Act 1988.

ISBN 978 1 4456 7885 6 (print)
ISBN 978 1 4456 7886 3 (ebook)

British Library Cataloguing in Publication Data.
A catalogue record for this book is available from
the British Library.

Origination by Amberley Publishing.
Printed in the UK.

Introduction

Although the articulated bus first appeared in service in the UK in June 1942 when four semi-trailer examples were built, it was not until 1977 that conventional bendy buses made their debut in Britain. Even then they failed to gain the same popularity they achieved in mainland Europe and several other parts of the world, and their total never reached four figures. During the early years of the Second World War, when the government was looking at schemes to increase capacity in the bus industry, it authorised the production of four buses using trailers attached to tractor units in a similar manner to today's semi-trailer articulated lorries. The first of these was completed in August 1941 and was shown to operators to seek their views. For a wide variety of reasons it failed to find favour and as a result in March 1942, after a further three artics had been built, it was stated at the Regional Traffic Commissioners' Conference that no further examples would be constructed. The four mentioned comprised two single-door thirty-eight-seat trailers built by British Trailer Corporation/Weymann that were hauled by Commer tractor units, and two constructed with two doors by Dyson/Roe, coupled to Bedford OXC tractor units. Because none of these buses met Construction & Use Regulations they were granted 'Special Types Authorisation', which permitted use in public service 'for experimental purposes only'. Thus, on 3 June 1942 the two Commers took up their revenue-earning duties with Mansfield & District Traction Co., while the Bedford duo were allocated to Liverpool Corporation, who employed them exclusively on a works service between Black Bull and Kirkby. While the latter used them until 1944, when they were converted to mobile staff canteens, the Mansfield pair, which had difficulty in maintaining timetables due to their restricted 20 mph speed limit, were taken out of service at an earlier date, after which they passed to Notts & Derby Electric Supply Company and remained with its successor, East Midlands Electricity Board, until the early 1960s. Despite the government's decision not to continue the construction of semi-trailer buses for public service, a number were, however, built for internal use at Royal Ordnance factories and other military installations. Then, after a rethink, the director general of mechanical equipment at the Ministry of Supply suggested in 1943 that a new generation of articulated buses could be built using existing single-deck bus chassis for motive power. To this end a pre-war AEC Regal had its chassis shortened to form a tractor unit and was coupled to a fifty-four-seat, two-door trailer built by British Trailers/MCW. This was demonstrated to operators, trade unions and the Ministry of War Transport on 17 February 1944, but was met with a hostile response, which led the government to quickly abandon the project in favour of building new bus bodies on conventional chassis, after which the AEC Regal was scrapped.

Following these experiments, it was to be more than thirty years before any further serious consideration was given to articulated buses in the UK, and even longer before they began to appear in quantity. South Yorkshire PTE was the first operator to show an interest in bendy buses when, in July 1977, it borrowed a left-hand drive Leyland-DAB-Saurer for demonstration purposes and followed it in October 1977 with a left-hand drive MAN SG192R. Then, in October 1978, a Stockholm Transport left-hand drive Volvo B58 bendy bus was examined by Eastern Scottish before spending a day on car park shuttle duties at the Commercial Motor Show at the NEC, in Birmingham.

It was, however, not until 29 March 1979 that bendy buses made their debut in public service in the UK when South Yorkshire PTE introduced five MAN SG192Rs. Leased from their manufacturer, they began operation on Sheffield's City Clipper service. Meanwhile, London Transport examined a Mercedes-Benz 0305G demonstrator, albeit to no avail, as no orders followed from the capital.

Returning to Sheffield, on 5 November 1979 South Yorkshire PTE borrowed a Leyland-DAB demonstrator, which it placed on the City Clipper service and obviously impressed, it leased a further four in the spring of 1980. Then, in May 1980, Morden-based Across Trust purchased three left-hand drive Van Hool TG821 bendy buses for use as Jumbulances, which were equipped with sixteen coach seats and fourteen beds for use on disabled people's holiday tours to Europe, and another was added in October 1985.

Moving forward to 1981, British Airways purchased seven Leyland-DAB bendy buses (fitted with Roe bodywork incorporating nearside and offside doors) for operation at Gatwick Airport, while in March of that year Luton Airport bought three left-hand drive Mercedes-Benz 0305Gs for airside use, following them soon afterwards with a further trio. Later in the year, on 17 September South Yorkshire PTE returned all its MAN and Leyland-DAB vehicles to their manufacturers, who then began to loan them to other operators in a bid to persuade them to purchase bendy buses. The MANs were loaned to City of Oxford, Ipswich Borough Council and Midland Red West before being sold to Midland Red North in January 1984, while one of the Leyland-DABs was evaluated by East Kent, Southend, Ipswich, Rossendale, East Yorkshire, Northern and Maidstone & District before two of them were sold to McGill's at Barrhead in 1983. Then, in 1986 Ensignbus purchased a second-hand, 1974-vintage, left-hand drive MAN SG192R for internal use at Gatwick Airport. After their evaluation had come to an end, four of the SYPTE MAN SG192Rs were sold to an Australian operator in Cairns, Queensland, with the fifth being sold for scrap, while two of its Leyland DABs found new lives in non-passenger carrying roles. It was not until 1994 that British Airways sold its Leyland DABs to Ensignbus, who removed the offside doors of one and prepared it for operation on London's Red Arrow services, for which its bid unfortunately failed. This was ultimately sold for a non-PSV role as were another two, while one was purchased by Ulsterbus, who used it as a driver trainer.

In the meantime, South Yorkshire PTE took the decision to venture back into bendy bus operation and on 22 August 1985 introduced thirteen Leyland-DABs (built to a new design) on the City Clipper service in Sheffield. In 1990, these were transferred onto a service from the city centre to the newly opened Meadowhall shopping complex. Then, for a few days in July 1991, SYPTE loaned one to Citybus, Belfast, for a shuttle service at the Tall Ships event, and in April 1992 loaned one to London Buses Selkent for evaluation on the 180 service from Greenwich to Abbey Wood. In the meantime, in April 1988, British Caledonian had purchased four Van Hool-bodied Volvo B10M-56s (with doors on both sides) for airside use at Gatwick, and later Luton, airports.

The next milestone in bendy bus operation in the UK came in 1992 when Southern Vectis borrowed a left-hand drive Mercedes-Benz 0405G, but quickly returned it after it was found to be unsuitable for the island. Following this, after thought had been given to building a guided busway in Bristol, in June Badgerline borrowed a left-hand drive, three-module Bombardier bendy bus from Rochefort, Belgium, which was later also tried out in Portsmouth. During the following month Go-Ahead Northern borrowed a Den Oudsten-bodied DAF SBR220, which, despite it being left-hand drive, was evaluated for several days on its service between Gateshead and the Metrocentre shopping complex. Before returning to its rightful owner, it was also examined in July by Dublin Bus and Belfast Citybus. Then, in November, Grampian Regional Transport purchased an Alexander-bodied Mercedes-Benz 0405G and placed it in service in Aberdeen. During the following year it undertook long-term evaluation with GRT Group companies Midland Bluebird and Leicester Citybus, into whose liveries it was repainted for the duration of its stays.

No further developments took place until May 1994 when Citybus, Belfast, placed two new Van Hool-bodied Volvo B10M-55s into service on its City Express operation. Having settled down and also spending some time being evaluated by Ulsterbus on a Gold Liner express service, in May 1996 Ulsterbus purchased two bendy buses of the same combination, albeit with coach seats. Then, after its subsidiary Fife Scottish had briefly trialled a South Yorkshire PTE Leyland-DAB, Stagecoach placed two new coach-seated Jonckheere-bodied Volvo B10M-55s in service with Fife Scottish on 12 July 1996, and a month later loaned one of them to its Oxford subsidiary for a fortnight's operation on the Oxford Tube service. In addition, during this same month (August), Stagecoach introduced ten new coach-seated Plaxton-bodied Volvo B10M-55s – four of which entered service with Ribble, three with Fife Scottish, two with Western Buses and one with Grimsby Cleethorpes – all of which were used on express services. However, after deciding to concentrate all its bendy buses in Scotland, in July 1997 Stagecoach transferred its Ribble and Grimsby Cleethorpes examples to Fife Scottish, to whom the Western Buses examples were also moved in January 1998.

During the spring of 1998, FirstBus loaned its Grampian Mercedes-Benz 0405G to First Leeds for three months for trials along the city's Scott Hall Road guided busway, and two months after it returned to Aberdeen on 24 May, it was loaned – for a second time – to First Leicester City Bus with whom it remained until September.

Finally, after bendy buses had been trialled by a handful of operators in various parts of the UK, in 1999 they now started to appear in quantity. The first to place them in service was Travel West Midlands, who purchased eleven Mercedes-Benz 0405GNs and put the first of them to work in Birmingham in February. Following them in

March were fifteen Wright-bodied Volvo B10LAs for First Manchester, who used them on a service from Manchester to Bury, while in May Stagecoach placed a further six Jonckheere-bodied Volvo B10M-55s in service – three of which were allocated to Cleveland Transit at Hull, with the remaining three joining Western Buses in Scotland. Then, in July, First Leeds began to progressively place fifteen buses of the same combination into service, with completion taking place in October, these being followed in November by a further ten making their debut with First Glasgow. As some new doors opened, however, one closed when, in July/August, Mainline in South Yorkshire withdrew all its Leyland-DABs without replacement, thus removing bendy buses from Sheffield. Despite their age, several found new owners, with three being acquired by Bath Bus Company, four crossing the water to Alan Martin Coaches in Dublin and one passing to Humberside Airport for airside duties.

In 2000, Volvo revised its B10LA model to become the B7LA, and finding bendy buses to be good 'crowd movers', FirstBus placed a further thirty-five in service – all with Wright bodies – with six in Aberdeen and eleven in Bradford in April, followed by eighteen in Southampton in August. For a couple of weeks in July, two of Aberdeen's bendis were loaned to First Edinburgh for trials, but apparently were not successful as no orders were placed. Prior to this, however, in March Citybus in Belfast had placed four dual-purpose-seated Mercedes-Benz O405GNs in service, while a month later Dublin Bus purchased a Wright-bodied Volvo B7LA for evaluation.

2001 began with Scania making its debut into the UK bendy bus market when, in February, First Manchester borrowed a Wright-bodied L94UA demonstrator for evaluation, and later purchased it. Then, following its successful trial, Dublin Bus placed a further twenty Wright-bodied Volvo B7LAs in service in March 2001, while during the following month Last Passive bought two buses of the same combination for use at Dublin Airport. Back in England, the first municipal bus operator to take an interest in bendy buses was Nottingham City Transport, who purchased a Wright-bodied Scania L94UA in June and a further two in November, although due to union problems none of these entered normal revenue-earning service until 17 June 2002, by which time a further two had been added to the fleet. After not previously showing an interest in bendy buses, Transport for London finally took the decision to conduct a trial, and on 15 October borrowed four Wright-bodied Volvo B10LAs from First Glasgow and two Wright-bodied Volvo B7LAs from First Southampton. These were operated by First Uxbridge Buses on the 207 service from Shepherds Bush to Hayes bypass from 15 October until 26 April of the following year, after which the Glasgow examples departed to join First Bristol at Bath and the Southampton pair were transferred to First Manchester. More surprising, however, was the first independent operator to purchase a bendy bus, this being Doig's of Glasgow, who in November took delivery of a Wright-bodied Scania L94UA for operation on an inter-campus service for Glasgow University. In November, yet another bus-builder entered the fray when Auwaeter supplied six Neoplan N2221S bendy buses to Meteor Parking at Stansted Airport, where they were employed on car park shuttle services. To speed up boarding and alighting, these buses had two doors in each of their modules and seating for twenty-eight passengers. Then, just before the year ended, in December

Go-Ahead Northern purchased four Wright-bodied Scania L94UAs for its service from Gateshead to the Metrocentre retail complex.

With the London trial obviously being regarded as successful, on 5 June 2002 Go-Ahead London General introduced thirty-one bendy buses on its Transport for London-contracted Red Arrow services, although these were Mercedes-Benz 0530Gs rather than Volvos. As will be seen later, these opened the flood gates in the capital, where bendy buses were to become a familiar sight. Meanwhile, in July 2002 Last Passive purchased three Mercedes-Benz 0530Gs for operation at Dublin Airport, while Stagecoach transferred its Cleveland Transit bendis, two of which had been loaned to Stagecoach Devon, to Western Buses, thus concentrating all its Volvo B10M-55s north of the border. FirstBus had also been moving its bendy buses around with some of its Glasgow examples being transferred to Bath, where they were used on a service to the city's university.

Having gained experience in London with its Red Arrow bendy buses, on 8 February 2003 Go-Ahead London Central introduced thirty Mercedes-Benz 0530Gs, leased from Lombard Leasing, on TfL's contracted 436 service from Paddington to Lewisham. A month later, on 15 March, Stagecoach Selkent placed thirty-two Mercedes-Benz 0530Gs, leased from Dawson Rentals, on TfL's route 453 between Marylebone and Deptford. This was not all, however, as on 15 November First London converted its 18 service to bendy bus operation with thirty-two Mercedes-Benz 0530Gs also leased from Dawson Rentals. Meanwhile, due to competition from FirstBus on its university service, in the spring Bath Bus Company withdrew its three ex-SYPTE Leyland DABs, selling one to Wigston independent operator Beaverbus and the other two to Ensign (dealer) at Purfleet. Then, in March First Bradford transferred six of its Volvo B10LAs to York, with three more following in April and its remaining two moving to Bath, while at around the same time all First Southampton's bendis were cascaded to First Glasgow. During May, Travel West Midlands introduced bendy buses to Coventry when it placed ten new Mercedes-Benz 0530Gs in service, while between July and October Menzies bought ten Scania CN94UAs for use on car park duties at London's Heathrow Airport. Later, in October, Meteor Parking purchased six new Mercedes-Benz 0530Gs for use on car park and staff shuttle duties at Stansted Airport. All was not well in London, however, as on 3 December one of Go-Ahead London Centrals 0530Gs was burnt out in service, while on 7 February and 20 March 2004 two more of its bendis suffered the same fate. As all three were write-offs, they were replaced with three new 0530Gs (which were given the same fleet numbers as those destroyed) between May and July 2004.

Earlier in 2004, a new Volvo B7LA demonstrator made its debut on extended loan to Go-Ahead London Central, this being uniquely fitted with a Hispano Habit body. On 24 April, the flood of Mercedes-Benz 0530G bendy buses into London continued when Arriva London North placed twenty-eight in service on route 149, followed on 26 June with Stagecoach East London introducing forty-two on the 25 service, the latter again being leased from Dawson Rentals. Then, continuing the 0530G flow into the capital, on 4 September Arriva London North put forty-eight into service on route 73, followed on 6 November by Go-Ahead London Central introducing thirty-three on South London route 12. Prior to this, Stagecoach had fitted three of its Plaxton-bodied Volvo B10M-55s with an onboard toilet and had repainted them into megabus.com livery for operation on its Glasgow to London service, while in June First Group-owned Last Passive (Aircoach) placed three new Mercedes-Benz 0530Gs in service at Dublin Airport to allow its three Volvo B7LAs to be transferred across the water to ultimately join First in Bath. In September, Travel West Midlands acquired eleven new Scania N94UAs for operation in Birmingham, their arrival allowing its Mercedes-Benz 0405Gs to be transferred to Coventry for further use. A month earlier, however, another bendy bus demonstrator made its debut, this being a hybrid Irisbus Civis, which was examined by Greater Manchester PTE for use on its proposed Leigh guided busway. In the event, the guided busway did not materialise until September 2013 and the Irisbus departed to its manufacturer without any particular interest having been shown. This was not the only demonstrator to appear, however, as in December a Scania N94UA took up its duties with Arriva London North on route 149 before ultimately passing on loan to Stagecoach East London, and then in 2005/6 to Go-Ahead Northern, Cardiff Bus and Lothian Buses.

2005 witnessed the arrival of another style of bendy bus when First Group introduced the 'ftr', a Volvo B7LA with Wright bodywork resembling a Las Vagas StreetCar. Of a striking new design, it had a separate cab for the driver and onboard self-service ticket machines, thus dispensing with the need for a conductor. A few days before the official launch at the Royal Naval College at Greenwich, London, on 10 March, the prototype had, however, undertaken a few trial journeys on the Monks Cross Park & Ride service in York, operated by FirstBus. Following this, First Manchester placed eighteen new Scania L94UAs in service in April, while a month later First Aberdeen added a further twenty new Wright-bodied Volvo B7LAs to its fleet, and in September First Somerset & Avon introduced nine new Wright-bodied Volvo B7LAs to its operations in Bath. In the meantime, more Mercedes-Benz 0530s had joined their sisters in London when, on 9 April, First London (CentreWest) converted its 207 service with twenty-seven buses leased from Dawson Rental, and Arriva London North placed forty-eight in service on the high-frequency 38 service. On 16 November, First Group demonstrated its prototype ftr in Edinburgh and Glasgow, although its lack of interest resulted in no forthcoming orders.

On 14 January 2006, the English capital completed its route conversion to bendy bus operation when Arriva London North introduced twenty-three Mercedes-Benz 0530Gs on the 29 service, and by this time no fewer than 396 0530Gs were in use in London, all on routes which entered the heart of the city. With bendy buses operating in England and Scotland, it was now time for Wales to join in the action, and to this end Cardiff Bus placed nineteen Scania N94UAs in service in May, wearing three different liveries. These were not the only surprise arrivals, as Cornwall independent Trunonian of Truro purchased three new Mercedes-Benz 0530Gs for operation on the car park shuttle at the Eden Centre. As one door opened, another one closed when, following the loss of a schools contract, Beaverbus sold its ex-SYPTE/Bath Bus Company Leyland DAB. Then, in September, Stagecoach sold its London bus operations to Australian Macquarie Bank, who renamed its new acquisition East London Bus & Coach Company.

Meanwhile, on 8 May FirstBus placed its first twelve ftrs in service in York, albeit not without numerous teething troubles. Finally, as the year drew to a close, Manchester Airport purchased the Hispano Habit-bodied Volvo B7LA demonstrator to test it on its public and staff car park shuttle services.

Moving forward to 2007, on 3 January First Leeds cautiously placed its first two ftrs into service on a cross-city route, and over the next few weeks progressively introduced a further fifteen. Due to 'kerb scrapes', however, their front wheel covers were soon removed, as too were those from the ftrs in York, and gradually they began to settle down in their new home. Not knowing where to operate its nine remaining ftrs, First put three to use on its First Capital Connect shuttle service at Luton Airport on 20 January 2008, while the balance remained in store. Prior to this, one of its ftrs had been demonstrated to Southend & Thurrock Council and First Cymru at Swansea, and had also, from 31 May, been loaned for two weeks to Go-Ahead Northern for trials on its Metrocentre service. Finding that the Hispano Habit had proved to be a useful tool on its car park shuttle services, Manchester Airport placed two new Mercedes-Benz 0530Gs in service in June, while Bristol Airport did likewise with two similar vehicles in September.

Although 2008 proved to be a comparatively quiet year, on 16 February Go-Ahead London Central won the contract for TfL route 453 from Stagecoach Selkent and purchased twenty-five new Mercedes-Benz 0530Gs for its operation. As a consequence, Stagecoach returned twenty-six of its 0530Gs to Dawson Rental, who then leased thirteen of them to CT Plus, Hackney, for use on the Olympic Park construction site, six to Arriva London North and one to First London. Later in the year, between October and January 2009, Last Passive purchased eleven new Mercedes-Benz 0530Gs for operation on Dublin Airport car park shuttle services.

January 2009 saw the arrival of seven new Mercedes-Benz 0530Gs with National Express at Stansted Airport and fifteen new 0530Gs with First York for Park & Ride duties, while on 1 June FirstBus finally placed its last five ftrs in service with First Cymru at Swansea, where they were joined by one transferred from Capital Connect at Luton Airport. Then, following a decree by the Mayor of London to rid the capital of its bendy buses, Go-Ahead London General's Red Arrow route 507 was withdrawn on 24 July, followed by Red Arrow 521 on 28 August, while Arriva London North's TfL 38 service was converted to conventional bus operation on 14 November. Now with surplus Mercedes-Benz 0530Gs, Go-Ahead London loaned one to Wilts & Dorset in September and one to Brighton & Hove for trials on its university services in October, these resulting in five being permanently transferred to the latter in February 2010. This, however, was not all, as knowing that it would have a surfeit of 0530Gs when further London withdrawals took place in 2010, in December Arriva London North loaned one to Isle of Man Transport for trials and transferred three to Arriva Merseyside.

2010 began with Dawson Rentals leasing four ex-Arriva London North 0530Gs to National Express at Stansted Airport, and then in May, Menzies placed eleven new Scania CN280UAs, leased from Dawson Rentals, in service at London's Heathrow Airport. Also in May/June, two of Arriva Merseyside's 0530Gs and two from Arriva

London North were transferred to Arriva Midlands at Leicester, while around this same time eleven of Arriva London North's 0530Gs were dispatched to Arriva Merseyside for further use in Liverpool. North of the border, in July Stagecoach surprisingly repainted five of its Plaxton-bodied Volvo B10M-55s into yellow school bus livery and transferred them to North Scotland, giving them yet another new role. Later in the year, on 15 October, Stagecoach repurchased its London operations from Macquarie Bank and thus regained its Mercedes-Benz 0530Gs employed on TfL route 25, while on the same day Arriva London North's TfL route 149 reverted to conventional operation, as too did First London's TfL route 18 on 12 November, thus further reducing bendy bus operation in the capital. Towards the end of the year, Dublin Bus had also begun to withdraw its bendy buses and completed the process in January 2011. Although all Dublin's Wright-bodied Volvo B7LAs crossed the water to dealers Ensign at Purfleet, while several were resold to Carlton breakers for scrapping, one was loaned in January to McGill's, Barrhead, for trial, while another was sold in March to Peoples Bus at Liverpool for further service.

In 2011, London finally bade farewell to its bendy buses when route 25 was converted to conventional bus operation on 25 June, followed by TfL route 73 on 3 September, route 12 on 5 November, the 29 on 26 November and First London-operated 207 on 10 December. As a result of all these withdrawals, new homes were sought for all the surplus 0530Gs and before long they began to appear in several new places. Single examples were loaned to Go-Ahead Northern, Plymouth and Dereham-based Konectbus, and while Plymouth appeared not to be impressed, Dawson Rentals leased twelve to CT Plus in Bristol where they were employed on Park & Ride duties. In November/December eleven were transferred from Go-Ahead London to Brighton & Hove, eight went to Go-Ahead Northern, twelve were cascaded to Go-South Coast's events fleet and five were acquired by Konectbus at Dereham. After being replaced by three First Somerset & Avon Wright-bodied Volvo B7LAs, Trunonian's three Mercedes-Benz 0530Gs were acquired by Hatfield-based UNO, while on 21 October Stagecoach fitted bunks to three of its magicbus.com Jonckheere-bodied Volvo B10M-55s for use on its new overnight sleeper coach service from Glasgow to London. More surprising, however, was the transfer of a large number of Arriva's London 0530Gs to its new subsidiary in Malta, where they entered service painted in Arriva's provincial UK livery. Of the eighty-six buses sent to the Mediterranean island between February 2011 and July 2013, some were only used for spares.

2012 saw the disposal of bendy buses continue, with two ex-Go-Ahead London Mercedes-Benz 0530Gs joining UNO at Hatfield in January, and two former Ulsterbus Van Hool-bodied Volvo B10M-55 being sold to independent operators in February, one each to Mortons, Little London and WJC Buses, Chapelhall. Then, in April, Clydeside operator McGill's purchased five ex-First London 0530Gs, while in May Leeds Bradford Airport bought three ex-Stagecoach London 0530Gs for airside use, these being followed in September by eight former Arriva London North 0530Gs crossing the water to Callinan, Claregalway, in Ireland, for operation on a construction workers' service in County Kildare. Leicestershire independent Beaverbus returned to the bendy bus fold when it bought five ex-Stagecoach London 0530Gs. Just before the year ended, McGill's acquired a further eleven ex-First London 0530Gs in December, but did not place them in service until April 2013. In the meantime, following a disagreement with York City Council, on 23 March First York withdrew its ftrs from the city and transferred them to First Leeds, where two were used and the remainder were placed in store. These were ultimately sent to an outside contractor for refurbishment and then on 28 October were returned to use on the ten-minute-frequency Hyperlink 72 service from Leeds to Bradford. These were not the only bendy buses to return to service, however, as in August Arriva London reinstated fifteen of its 0530Gs on London Olympics Hospitality Centre duties. On the flip side, during the year Menzies withdrew all its Heathrow Scania CN94UAs.

Yet another eventful year, 2013 saw several ex-London 0530Gs loaned or sold to a variety of operators. In February, Isle of Man Transport borrowed a trio of Arriva London North examples for further evaluation, while in May a Go-Ahead London bendy bus was loaned for a week to Ipswich Buses – all to no avail, however, as none of these undertakings were persuaded to purchase any. Then, in March, three of Go-Ahead London's buses were acquired by Blackpool independent Catch 22, who on 4 October placed them on its new, short-lived Red Rocket service from the seaside resort to Manchester, which only lasted until 20 December. Not all of the bendy buses were so fortunate, however, as following a number of fires, the Maltese Government instructed Arriva to immediately take all its 0530Gs out of service at the end of August, and as a consequence they never returned to use. All were sold to the Maltese Government when it took over Arriva's operations on 1 January 2014 and although they were reportedly resold to a buyer in Sudan, the deal was cancelled and all were subsequently disposed of for scrapping. Meanwhile, in the UK withdrawals continued with McGill's taking its original five 0530Gs out of service, Konectbus selling three 0530Gs to EvoBus (dealers) in June and Go-South Coast starting to rid itself of its 0530Gs, while between December and February 2014 Go-Ahead Northern disposed of fourteen 0530Gs to Optare at Sherburn-in-Elmet. Of the latter, Optare sold six to Brighton & Hove and two to a Cypriot buyer. These were not the only 0530Gs originating in London to find new homes in North Cyprus, as North East University bought more than twenty-five, Cyprus International University acquired five and the European University of Lefke took two or three, all of which were used on student shuttle services. Then, although Manchester Airport purchased four ex-First London 0530Gs, it took two of its original 0530Gs out of service and retained one of them, placing it on display at its Aviation Viewing Park. Prior to this, the scrapping of bendy buses in the UK continued apace, with several ex-First Leeds and First Manchester Volvo B10LAs and former London Mercedes-Benz 0530Gs being reduced to tangled metal by PVS and Ripley at Carlton, as well as ex-First Glasgow Volvo B10LAs at Alpha Recovery's Weetslade premises.

Over the next four years, further withdrawals took place, starting in July 2014 when Nottingham City Transport ceased bendy bus operation, as too did Arriva Merseyside. Then, on 31 January 2015 Go-North East withdrew the last of its Mercedes-Benz 0530Gs, while on 28 August 2015 First Cymru took its small fleet of ftrs out of service, only to temporarily reinstate two in September when extra capacity was needed on the route serving the city's university. Following this, First Leeds withdrew all its ftrs in July 2016 when the 72 service between Bradford to Leeds was converted to double-deck operation, and two months later CT Plus at Bristol took its 0530s out of service after it lost its Park & Ride contracts in the city. Next to abandon bendy bus operation was First Manchester, who withdrew its fleet in August 2017, then, finally, National Express Coventry on 20 March 2018. Of the latter, however, towards the end of the year two were fortunate enough to find a new operational home with Somerset Passenger Solutions, while the remainder were dispatched to the breaker's yards.

Proving that bendy buses are not yet dead, however, Ulster's national operator Translink introduced thirty new 18-metre-long diesel-hybrid Van Hool Exquiciti vehicles on its new Belfast Rapid Transit operation, upon which trial passenger-carrying runs began on 28 August 2018, with the full service starting on 3 September. Meanwhile, in 2017 Bristol Airport had purchased two new Mercedes Benz 0295Gs in May 2017 and a further example in October 2018 while OFS connections at Gatwick Airport had bought seven in June 2017.

Out of the 858 bendy buses that have been operated in the UK since 1979, around 250 have been exported, while at the end of 2018 no fewer than 116 were still in revenue-earning service in the UK: thirty in Belfast; thirteen at First Aberdeen; fourteen at First Somerset & Avon in Bath; twenty-two with Brighton & Hove; nineteen at Cardiff Bus; one at Konectbus; two with Somerset Passenger Solutions; and fifteen with First York. In addition, of course, are the bendies employed on car park and airside duties at various UK and Irish airports, plus a tiny handful that have gained a new life in preservation.

Despite the fact that many enthusiasts might find the bendy bus does not capture their particular interest, it is nevertheless an important part of Britain's transport history and worthy of examination, and as such I hope that this book will illustrate its presence and recapture memories of these non-conventional buses across our native shores.

Without the help of numerous others, it would not have been possible to compile this history or illustrate bendy buses in so many different locations, and I am particularly grateful to all the photographers who have generously allowed me to use their work. Where known each is credited in the photographic caption, but unfortunately many remain anonymous and thus I sincerely apologise for being unable to name them. I hope that they will forgive me for this but will, however, enjoy seeing their work in print, for without them this book would have been much less comprehensive.

Bendy Buses Operated in the UK and Ireland

Make/Model	Into Service	Total
Leyland-DAB	1979–85	25
MAN SG192R (2*)	1979–81	7
Mercedes-Benz 0305G*	1981	6
Mercedes-Benz 0405G	1992	1

Mercedes-Benz 0405GN	1999–2000	15
Mercedes-Benz 0530G	2002–09	479
Mercedes-Benz 0295G	2017–18	10
Neoplan N4421	2001	6
Scania CN94UA	2003	10
Scania CN280UA	2010	11
Scania L94UA	2001–02	11
Scania N94UA	2004	49
Van Hool Exquicity	2018	30
Van Hool T821*	1980–85	4
Volvo B7LA	2000–07	128
Volvo B10LA	1998–99	40
Volvo B10M-55	1994–96	16
Volvo B10MA-55	1999	6
Volvo B10M-56	1988	4
		858

*Left-hand drive

One of the pair of British Trailer Corporation/Weymann-bodied Commer semi-trailer style articulated buses supplied to Mansfield & District in 1942. (Autobus Library)

Seen outside the Crossgates factory of Chas H. Roe in 1942 is one of the two Bedford OXC semi-trailer buses supplied to Liverpool Corporation. (Autobus Library)

Built by British Trailers/MCW in 1944 and fitted to a shortened pre-war AEC Regal chassis, this attempt at producing an articulated bus failed at the first hurdle and was never placed in service. (Autobus Library)

The first bendy bus to be demonstrated in the UK was this left-hand drive Leyland-DAB-Saurer, seen on trade plates in Sheffield in July 1977 with South Yorkshire PTE. (Autobus Library)

Another bendy bus demonstrated to South Yorkshire PTE and later placed in service numbered 2006 was MAN SG192R CLM 346T, pictured here in September 1978. (Autobus Library)

With trade plates in its windscreen, Stockholm Transport's Van Hool-bodied Volvo B58 5394 is seen being demonstrated at Gosforth Park, Newcastle-upon-Tyne, on 7 October 1978. (T. W. W. Knowles)

One of four Van Hool-bodied Volvo B10M-56s operated by British Caledonian, 12 (E668 FLD) is seen here at Luton Airport. (Author's collection)

Although registered in the UK, the four Van Hool TG821s operated as Jumbulance sleeper coaches by Across Trust were of left-hand drive configuration due to them being operated mainly in continental Europe. Here, NPF 694W is seen at its home base.(Author's collection)

The first bendy bus to be acquired for preservation in the UK was this ex-Aachen, Germany, left-hand drive MAN SG192R, AC-L-497, seen here in Halifax in 1987. (K. A. Jenkinson)

Surprisingly seen here in Manchester's Piccadilly bus station while on a promotional tour, and clearly showing its offside doors, is British Airways Leyland-DAB BU310 (RLN 237W). (Author's collection)

One of six all-white liveried left-hand drive Mercedes-Benz 0305Gs purchased by Luton Airport for use on airside duties, 3 (UBH 396W), with rear wheel spats, is seen undertaking its role in 1985. (M. H. A. Flynn)

Seen at Rush Green Motors (dealer) after serving at Luton Airport is another of its Mercedes-Benz 0305G airside bendy buses. (Author's collection)

Still wearing South Yorkshire PTE livery, fleet number 2010 and Cityliner identity, Leyland-DAB FHE 293V additionally carries an East Kent fleet name and NBC logo on its side panels while on loan to that company in September 1983. (T. S. Blackman)

Still in South Yorkshire PTE livery but now sporting a Reddibus fleet name, MAN SG192R 2004 (DAK 204V) is seen here in Redditch while operating on loan to Midland Red West in 1983. (K. Jubb)

Still retaining its offside doors, ex-British Airways Roe-built Leyland-DAB RLN 235W is seen here at Rosslare Harbour, Eire, while being used by Stena Line on dockside transfer duties. (Darren Hall)

Having ended its life as a driver trainer with Ulsterbus and no longer having offside doors, former British Airways Leyland-DAB 2999 (RLN 234W) awaits its fate in the yard of its owner's Newtownabbey depot on 15 September 2002. (K. A. Jenkinson)

Acquired by Stagecoach Hampshire Bus from McGill's, Barrhead, Leyland-DAB FHE 291V, which was new to South Yorkshire PTE, is seen operating a service in Winchester. (K. A. Jenkinson)

Seen while being evaluated by Ipswich Borough Council, South Yorkshire PTE MAN SG192R 2005 (CLM 346T) squeezes between a variety of the municipal's buses while operating service 13 to Chantry Estate. (Author's collection)

Repainted in Midland Red North Chaserider livery, former South Yorkshire PTE MAN SG192R DAK 301V is pictured operating the car park shuttle service at the National Exhibition Centre, Birmingham, in October 1984. (K. A. Jenkinson)

In 1994, former British Airways Leyland-DAB RLN 233W was repainted by Capital Citybus in anticipation of gaining the contract to operate the London Buses 507 Red Arrow service, which, in the event, it failed to achieve. (Author's collection)

Sadly, the original MAN SG192R demonstrator, CLM 346T, ended its life in the yard of Wigley (breaker), Carlton, where it is seen, partly scrapped, in March 1988. (T. Wigley & Son)

Seen at the West of England Transport Collection's premises at Winkleigh after its life with Wirral Metropolitan Borough Council had ended is now preserved ex-South Yorkshire PTE prototype Leyland-DAB CRM 927T, while in the distance is the preserved front module of Leyland-DAB RLN 237W, which had served as a playbus but began life with British Airways. (C. Shears)

Resting at London Gatwick Airport in May 1987 while being used as an airside bus is KTW 375N, a left-hand drive MAN SG192R owned by Ensignbus, Purfleet. (F. W. York)

Seen in its home city, Leyland-DAB 2006 (C106 HDT) has had South Yorkshire Transport (SYT) logos added to its original Clipper livery. (K. S. E. Till)

Departing from Meadowhall, Sheffield, on 22 October 1992, coach-seated Leyland-DAB 2011 (C111 HDT), which had no door in its rear module, is seen displaying Rotherham Mainline fleet names. (K. A. Jenkinson)

As can be seen, the bus-seated Leyland-DABs had three doors, whereas the bus-seated variants had no doors in their rear module. Here, 2007 (C107 HDT) carries a dedicated livery for the Meadowhall Express 501 service, upon which it is seen leaving the bus/rail interchange at the retail complex. (K. A. Jenkinson)

During its period on loan to London Buses, Sheffield Mainline Leyland-DAB C101 HDT retained its rightful owner's livery but was given Selkent fleet names and a London bulls-eye logo. It is seen here at Manor Way, Abbey Wood, on 18 April 1992. (Nigel Eadon-Clarke)

Collecting its Metrocentre-bound passengers at Gateshead Interchange in July 1992 is this left-hand drive Dutch DAF SBR220 bendy bus, which was trialled by Go-Ahead Northern, who gave it temporary fleet number 7771. (Autobus Library)

Seen demonstrating its capabilities in Portsmouth on 26 June 1992 was this left-hand drive Belgian Bombardier diesel-electric three-module bendy bus. (T. W. W. Knowles)

New in May 1994 to Citybus, Belfast, and branded for the City Express services, Van Hool-bodied Volvo B10M-55 3000 (DAZ 3000) is seen here resting at its owner's Newtownabbey depot in September 1995. (K. A. Jenkinson)

One of the ex-South Yorkshire PTE MAN SG192Rs is seen here in its new home in Cairns, Queensland, Australia, in 1987. (Author's collection)

Four ex-First Mainline Leyland-DABs ultimately found a new home across the water in Dublin with Cloncilla-based Alan Martin Coaches, with whom they are seen here in July 2007 still carrying their English registration marks: C105/7/6/1 HDT. (Darren Hall)

The first Mercedes-Benz 0405G articulated bus to enter service in Britain was Grampian Regional Transport's Alexander-bodied 1 (K1 GRT), which was new in November 1992. (Autobus Library)

Stagecoach Fife Scotland's Jonckheere-bodied Volvo B10M-55 562 (N562 SJF), which was new in June 1996, is seen here leaving Buchanan bus station, Glasgow, on an X25 journey to Aberhill on 3 September 1999. (K. A. Jenkinson)

Seen in Preston bus station running on trade plates while undertaking driver training in August 1996 is Stagecoach Ribble's new Plaxton-bodied Volvo B10M-55 101 (P973 UBV). (K. A. Jenkinson)

Displaying route branding for the over-ground route 8 between Bolton and Manchester, First Manchester Wright-bodied Volvo B10LA 10003 (S994 UJA) is captured passing Manchester Victoria railway station on 24 March 2007. (M. H. A. Flynn)

First Southampton Wright-bodied Volvo B7LA 143 (X143 FPO) with overground identity and route branding on its cove panels is seen here at the Showbus event at Duxford on 28 September 2003. (R. G. Pope)

Seen on 20 May 2000 leaving Holt Park on route 1 to Beeston, for which it carries branding on its cove panels, is First Leeds Wright-bodied Volvo B10LA 1104 (T104 VWU). (K. A. Jenkinson)

Resting at its home depot on 24 July 2002 is First Bradford Wright-bodied Volvo B7LA 1124 (W124 DWX), seen wearing Sovereign branding above the rear wheel arch of its front module and route details on its cove panels. (K. A. Jenkinson)

First Glasgow Wright-bodied Volvo B7LA 10149 (Y149 ROT), seen here on 25 March 2008, began life south of the border with First in Southampton. (M. H. A. Flynn)

Dublin Bus's first bendy bus, Wright Eclipse Fusion-bodied Volvo B7LA 00-D-31079, is seen when new in 2000, still wearing its silver demonstration livery. (Darren Hall)

Grampian's Alexander-bodied Mercedes-Benz 0405G K1 GRT is seen here repainted into Midland Bluebird's GRT-style livery while on loan to that company for evaluation in 1993. (Autobus Library)

The first bendy bus to be purchased by an independent operator was Wright-bodied Scania L94UB SJ51 LPA, which was used by Doig's, Glasgow, on a service to Strathclyde University, and is seen here in November 2012. (Richard Walter)

The much-travelled First Aberdeen Mercedes-Benz 0405G K1 GRT is seen here displaying First logos while on loan to First Leicester Citybus in June 1998. (Author's collection)

Travel West Midlands' first bendy bus, Mercedes-Benz 0405GN 6001 (S1 TWM), which was new in February 1999, is seen in September of that year, adorned with branding for route 67 and proudly displaying its articulated credentials. (R. G. Pope)

Also new in 1999 (in May) was Stagecoach Cleveland Transit Jonckheere-bodied Volvo B10MA-55 97 (T97 JHN), which was branded for the Hull to Sheffield 909 service. Before the end of the year, it was transferred north of the border, where Stagecoach concentrated all its bendies. (R. G. Pope)

Painted in Unilink livery, Nottingham City Transport Wright-bodied Scania L94UA 704 (FE02 AKV) is seen in April 2008 on the service to Nottingham Trent University. (R. G. Pope)

Parked in its owner's Broadstone depot in September 2002 is Dublin Bus Wright-bodied Volvo B7LA AW2 (00-D-65002), which was new in April 2001. (K. A. Jenkinson)

New in May 2000, First Aberdeen's 'Barbie-liveried' Wright-bodied Volvo B7LA 10049 (W4 FAL) is pictured here resting between duties at its owner's depot on 30 June 2005. (Barry Newsome)

Adorned with City Express branding, Citybus Belfast's dual-purpose-seated Mercedes-Benz 0405GN 3100 (DCZ 3100), which was new in March 2000, is seen here at Newtownabbey depot on 21 April 2001. (K. A. Jenkinson)

Starting life in February 2001 as a demonstrator, Wright-bodied Scania L94UA X401 CSG was then purchased by First Manchester, with whom it is seen here in Bury, numbered 10017. (M. H. A. Flynn)

Following its sale by Bath Bus Company to RML Travel for non-PSU promotional use, BBZ 6818 (originally C113 HDT) was acquired by Stafford Bus Centre (dealer), at whose Cotes Heath premises it is seen in October 2009, before being resold for preservation. (K. A. Jenkinson)

The only Neoplan N4221 bendy buses to be operated in the UK were those used at Stansted Airport by Meteor Parking, whose B6 (YN51 XLZ), which was new in November 2001, is seen here undertaking car park shuttle duties in July 2002. (Author's collection)

Pictured at the Metrocentre while operating the X66 express shuttle service from Gateshead when less than a year old is Go-Ahead Northern Wright-bodied Scania L94UA 4951 (NK51 OLT), which entered service in December 2001. (Mark Harrington)

Leaving Victoria bus station on 2 June 2006, en route to Waterloo on Red Arrow service 507, is Go-Ahead London General Mercedes-Benz 0530G MAL16 (BX02 YYW). (R. G. Pope)

Awaiting its departure from Euston Square to Sudbury on route 18 is First CentreWest Mercedes-Benz 0530G EA11011 (LK53 FBE). (M. H. A. Flynn)

Circumnavigating Parliament Square while operating the 453 service to Deptford on 17 May 2003 is Stagecoach Selkent Mercedes-Benz 0530G 23021 (LX03 HDE). (K. A. Jenkinson)

Collecting its Lewisham-bound passengers on route 436 on 2 June 2006 is Go-Ahead London Central Mercedes-Benz 0530G MAL33 (BN52 GWD). (R. G. Pope)

Having been transferred to First York from Bradford and repainted into a dedicated livery for its new home city's Park & Ride services, upon which it is seen here on 8 August 2008, is Wright-bodied Volvo B7LA 10041 (W124 DWX), which was seen in its original home earlier in the book. (K. A. Jenkinson)

Passing Coventry Transport Museum on 7 October 2006 is West Midlands Travel Coventry's route 27-branded Mercedes-Benz 0530G 6020 (BJ03 ETK), which leaves its passengers in no doubt that it is a bendy bus. (R. G. Pope)

Seen in August 2003 on delivery to Menzies at London's Heathrow Airport for car park shuttle duties is an as yet unregistered Scania CN94UA. (Scania)

When evaluated in Edinburgh, the unique Hispano-bodied Volvo B7LA demonstrator FJ53 LZX had harlequin and Lothian logos added to its London red livery. (Richard Walter)

Arriva London North Mercedes-Benz 0530G MA89 (BX55 FWA) passes King's Cross railway station on its way to Stoke Newington on 28 June 2011. (M. H. A. Flynn)

One of several London Mercedes-Benz 0530Gs that were given all-over advertising liveries, Stagecoach Selkent 23034 (LX03 HEU), seen here making its way through Piccadilly on a 453 journey to Deptford, wears one promoting the University of East London. (D. W. Rhodes)

Bound for Dulwich Library on route 12, Go-Ahead London Central Mercedes-Benz 0530G MAL88 (BX54 UDV) picks up some passengers in Whitehall on 16 October 2011. (K. A. Jenkinson)

New in November 2004 as a demonstrator for its manufacturer, Scania N94UA YN54 ALO is seen here being evaluated by Lothian Buses, who repainted it into their Park & Ride livery and gave it temporary fleet number 50. (Richard Walter)

Seen converted into an overnight sleeper coach for the Glasgow to London service and repainted in megabus.com livery is Stagecoach West Scotland Jonckheere-bodied Volvo B10M-55 51062 (SJI 1631, originally N562 SJF). (Stagecoach)

Scania N94UA demonstrator YN54 ALO is seen here being evaluated by Stagecoach East London on route 25. (Author's collection)

Branded for route 67, Travel West Midlands Scania N94UA 6024 (BX54 DNE) clearly shows its bendy credentials in Birmingham city centre on 18 November 2006. (R. G. Pope)

Following the arrival of Travel West Midlands' new Scania N94UAs in Birmingham, its Mercedes-Benz 0405Gs were transferred to its Coventry operation, where 6009 (T609 MOA) is seen on 7 October 2006 wearing Prime Lines and route 21 branding. (R. G. Pope)

Standing in front of a Stagecoach Magicbus Leyland Olympian while being demonstrated to Greater Manchester PTE in August 2004 is this French Irisbus Civis bendy bus. (Barry Newsome)

Starting life in December 2003 as a demonstrator for Evobus, Coventry, Mercedes-Benz BU53 ZWV was later sold to Manchester Airport, with whom it is seen here in April 2011 with trade plates at the lower edge of its windscreen. (M. H. A. Flynn)

BN02 EDN, which carries a personalised registration plate removed from a Transbus Enviro 300, was one of three Mercedes-Benz 0530Gs bought new by independent Trunonian for operation on the Eden Project Park & Ride service. (Author's collection)

Running on trade plates, and seen here behind York Racecourse at the First York ftr launch on 8 May 2006, is the prototype which was later given fleet number 19000 and registered YK06 CZN before ultimately becoming S90 FTR at Swansea with First Cymru. (K. A. Jenkinson)

Carrying branding for route 135 on its cove panels, First Manchester Scania L94UA 12004 (YN05 GYJ) crawls in heavy traffic past the city's Arndale shopping complex on 21 April 2012. (M. H. A. Flynn)

New to First Somerset & Avon and painted in a dedicated livery for services to Bath University is Wright-bodied Volvo B7LA 10179 (WX55 HWE), seen here on 1 September 2009. (R. G. Pope)

Arriving at Trafalgar Square at the end of its route 29 journey from Wood Green in September 2010 is Arriva London North MA144 (BX55 FXH). (K. A. Jenkinson)

Leaving Buchanan bus station, Glasgow, on 13 October 2007 is Stagecoach West Scotland Plaxton-bodied Volvo B10M-55 51076 (MSU 466, originally P976 UBV), which was new to Stagecoach Ribble. It is seen here branded for the X76 service to Cumnock. (M. H. A. Flynn)

Resting in its owner's depot on 16 June 2007 is Cardiff Buses Baycar-branded Scania N94UA 603 (CN06 GDO). (R. G. Pope)

Wearing an attractive red, orange and turquoise livery with Cardiff Red branding for services 17 and 18 to Ely is Cardiff Bus Scania N94UA 608 (CN06 GDU), caught by the camera on 27 June 2006. (R. G. Pope)

Painted in a generic livery, Cardiff Buses Scania N94UA 618 (CN06 GDX) passes through Cardiff city centre on 12 August 2012. (R. G. Pope)

One of four ex-London Mercedes-Benz 0530Gs owned by Last Bus, Brannockstown (who trade as Dublin Coach), 03-KE-16220 is seen operating a car park shuttle service at Dublin Airport on 24 August 2016. This bus began life with First CentreWest, with whom it was registered LK53 FCO. (Paul Savage)

Callinan of Galway's Mercedes-Benz 530G 05-G-16966, seen here in January 2013, still wears the livery of Arriva London North, from whom it was acquired, and with whom it was numbered MA84 and registered BU05 VFG. (Darren Hall)

Only operating for Go-North East for a short time, and never repainted out of its Go-London Central livery, 5357 (BX54 UCO) is seen in Newcastle-upon-Tyne on the 58 service to Hadrian Park in 2012. (Northeastbuses)

With London's Royal Exchange forming the backdrop, East London Bus & Coach Company's freshly repainted Mercedes-Benz 0530G 23072 (LX04 LCN) heads to Tottenham Court Road station on route 25 in October 2010 – a few days before reverting back to Stagecoach ownership. (K. A. Jenkinson)

Seen at York railway station, Wright ftr-bodied Volvo B7LA 19003 (YK06 ATU), still with its front wheel covers fitted, collects its university-bound passengers on route 4. (K. A. Jenkinson)

Painted in an all-over livery designed by a graphic art student at Leeds Metropolitan University, First York Wright ftr-bodied Volvo B7LA 19001 (YK06 AOU) passes the city's railway station on its first day in service, 8 May 2006. (K. A. Jenkinson)

Seen in May 2012 operating a staff shuttle service is Manchester Airport's unique Hispano-bodied Volvo B7LA FJ53 LZX, which had started life in February 2004 as a demonstrator for Volvo. (M. H. A. Flynn)

First Leeds Wright 'ftr'-bodied Volvo B7LA 19024 (YJ07 LVS), with branding for cross-city route 4 on its cove panels, is seen here in Leeds City Square in October 2013. (K. A. Jenkinson)

Starting life at Dublin Airport with Last Passive registered 01-D-76812, and later transferred to First Capital Connect, with whom it is seen here at Luton Airport on 15 August 2009, is Mercedes-Benz 0530G 11035 (T5 FCC). (John Podgorski)

New to First Leeds registered YJ07 LVX, but immediately transferred to First Capital Connect for use on the service from Luton Parkway railway station to Luton Airport, 19031 was re-registered T6 FCC for its new role and is seen here on 2 April 2013 adorned with appropriate branding. (M. A. Penn)

Adorned with an all-over contravision advert, Manchester Airport Mercedes-Benz 0530G BX07 NMF was purchased new in June 2007 and is seen here on 11 May 2012 leaving the terminal on a car park shuttle service. (M. H. A. Flynn)

Seen here on the red car park shuttle service at Dublin Airport on 24 August 2016 is Last Passive Mercedes-Benz 0530G 11083 (09-D-5303), which was purchased new in January 2009. (Paul Savage)

Dropping off its car park passengers at Stansted Airport in March 2013 is National Express Mercedes-Benz 0530G SA07 (KX58 GUH), which had been bought new in January 2009. (Author's collection)

Pictured in Norwich on 17 August 2013 is Konectbus Mercedes-Benz 0530G 802 (BD57 WCZ), which originated with London General in February 2008. (John Podgorski)

Seen in Swansea city centre, First Cymru Wright ftr-bodied Volvo B7LA 19033 (S80 FTR) started life registered YN07 SYJ. (Author's collection)

Seen on 26 March 2008 after Go-Ahead London Central took over TfL route 453 from East London Bus & Coach Co., Mercedes-Benz 0530G MAL100 (BD57 WDK) is seen here awaiting its departure from Marylebone. (R. G. Pope)

Operating one of the city's Park & Ride services in June 2009 is First York Mercedes-Benz 11110 (BG58 OME), seen painted in the dedicated livery applied to all the buses used on these duties. (M. H. A. Flynn)

With its fleet names removed, Arriva London North Mercedes-Benz 0530G MA38 (BX04 NEF) is seen while on loan to Isle of Man Transport. (R. Dodge)

The last new Scania bendy buses to be placed in service in the UK were eleven CN280UAs with Menzies, Heathrow – one of which, SA9 (YT10 OBJ), which was new in May 2010, is seen here at London's Heathrow Airport. (Author's collection)

Two of Arriva Merseyside's ex-Arriva London North Mercedes-Benz 0530Gs – 6024 (BX04 MXZ) and 6013 (BX04 MXL) – are seen here on the 699 service to Liverpool University's halls of residence on 21 September 2011. (L. J. Long)

Leaving Liverpool Airport en route to the city centre on 7 September 2011, and painted into a dedicated livery for the AirLink 501 service, is Arriva Merseyside's Mercedes-Benz 0530G 6005 (BX04 MXB), which had started life with Arriva London North in three-door configuration. (K. A. Jenkinson)

Acquired by First Group from Ensign (dealer), Purfleet, albeit only for spares, were Dublin Bus Volvo B7LAs AW13 (00-D-65013) and AW19 (00-D-65019). Here they are seen being stripped on First's behalf in the yard of PVS (breaker), Carlton, on 17 August 2011. (K. A. Jenkinson)

After serving as a megabus.com coach, Stagecoach East Scotland Plaxton-bodied Volvo B10M-55 51070 (DSV 943, originally P670 LWB) is seen after being relegated to school duties, for which it was given a dedicated yellow livery. (Murdoch Currie)

Seen at Ensign (dealer), Purfleet, on 3 April 2011 having been prepared for McGill's, Greenock, in whose livery it had been repainted, is ex-Dublin Bus Wright-bodied Volvo B7LA X945 CNO (originally 00-D-65016). To its left is sister 00-D-65002, which sadly failed to find a buyer and was disposed of for scrap. (John Podgorski)

Having evaluated a South Yorkshire PTE MAN SG192R bendy bus two decades earlier, here in the summer of 2013 we see Go-Ahead London Central Mercedes-Benz 0530G BX54 UDJ on loan to Ipswich Buses, which has given it temporary fleet number 500. (Author's collection)

Apart from the Dublin Bus Volvo B7LA loaned to McGill's, the only other example to find a new operational home was 00-D-65007, which was re-registered X958 CNO and acquired in March 2011 by Liverpool independent Peoplesbus, who then gave it a personal registration: X1 BUS. (Peoplesbus)

New to Stagecoach Western Scottish, Plaxton-bodied Volvo B10M-55 P198 OSE is seen here with Leicestershire independent Reliant Coaches but was later sold on to Seaford & District at Lewes. (Author's collection)

Leicestershire independent Beaverbus of Whetstone's ex-Stagecoach East London Mercedes-Benz 0530G LX04 LCM is seen here operating a school bus duty. (Author's collection)

Painted in a dedicated livery for the 904 Park & Ride service in Bristol is CT Plus Mercedes-Benz 0530G MCA18 (BX02 YZT), which was new to Go-Ahead London General and used on Red Arrow services. (Author's collection)

Seen operating Park & Ride service 902 in Bristol is CT Plus Mercedes-Benz 0530G MCA23 (BX02 YYS), which was new to Go-Ahead London General. (Author's collection)

Painted in a yellow livery for operation on Park & Ride services in Bristol is CT Plus Mercedes-Benz 0530G MCA13 (BX02 YZG), which also began life with Go-Ahead London General on Red Arrow services. (Author's collection)

Seen in Bath operating for First Somerset & Avon on its university services, Wright-bodied Volvo B7LA 10153 (Y642 AVV) began life with Last Passive, Dublin (registered 01-D-38300), whose livery it still carries here. (Barry Newsome)

Adorned in a dedicated livery for the city's university services, First Leeds Wright-bodied Volvo B7LA 10043 (W129 DWX) awaits its passengers at Leeds railway station on 9 January 2012. (K. A. Jenkinson)

New to First Somerset & Avon, but seen here at Luton Airport Parkway railway station on 27 July 2010 after transfer to First Capital Connect, is Wright-bodied Volvo B7LA 10180 (T3 FCC, originally WX55 HWF). (Author's collection)

Although branded for route 25, Brighton & Hove's Mercedes-Benz 0530G 112 (BD57 WDR) is seen here operating a football special to Brighton & Hove Albion's stadium on 29 September 2012. It had begun life with Go-Ahead London General in February 2008 and has been converted from three to two-door configuration. (T. S. Blackman)

Cascaded from Go-Ahead London Central to Go-Ahead Northern, Mercedes-Benz 0530G 5355 (BX54 UDB), painted in Citylink-branded livery, is seen here in Newcastle-upon-Tyne on 4 November 2013 while operating cross-city service 54 to Heworth. (Richard Walter)

Operating the X40 Park & Ride service in Newcastle-upon-Tyne on 4 November 2013 is Go-North East Wright-bodied Scania L94UA 4952 (NK51 OLU), which was purchased new in December 2001. (Richard Walter)

New to Trunonian registered BN02 EDN, and pictured earlier in this book, Universitybus (UNO) of Hatfield Mercedes-Benz MBA 326 is seen in Luton on 30 October 2012 after being re-registered MH06 JYE. (M. A. Penn)

Still wearing its former owner's livery (First CentreWest), but now sporting the fleet name of its new owner (Manchester Airport), Mercedes-Benz 0530G LK53 FCM is pictured in its new home on a staff shuttle service on 13 August 2014. (M. H. A. Flynn)

Pictured at Londonderry in January 2012 after being transferred to Ulsterbus and repainted into its blue and white livery is ex-Metro, Belfast, Mercedes-Benz 0405GN 3103 (DCZ 3103). (Paul Savage)

Ulsterbus Van Hool-bodied Volvo B10M-55 3112 (JAZ 3002) is also seen here at Londonderry, albeit in September 1996, painted in Goldliner livery. (K. A. Jenkinson)

Repainted into Arriva corporate livery and seen at London Bus & Truck, Northfleet, on 22 August 2011, having been prepared for transfer to Arriva Malta, where it was to be registered BUS 258, is Arriva London North Mercedes-Benz 0530G MA157 (BX55 FXY). (D. W. Rhodes)

New to Arriva London North as its MA146, Arriva Malta Mercedes-Benz 0530G BUS 248 is seen here in Bugibba bus station in July 2011 displaying route branding above the side windows of its front module. (K. S. E. Till)

Collecting its passengers in Victoria bus station, Gozo, in July 2011, Arriva Malta Mercedes-Benz 0530G BUS 216 started life in the UK with Arriva London North, in whose fleet it was numbered MA102 (BX55 FVB). (K. S. E. Till)

Wearing an anonymous white livery when photographed in October 2012, Arriva Malta Mercedes-Benz 0530G BUS 706 (originally Arriva London North MA76) was later repainted into corporate colours. (K. S. E. Till)

Having crossed the water from Ulsterbus in Northern Ireland, Van Hool-bodied Volvo B10MA-55 H15 BUS (originally DAZ 3001) found a new home with Hampshire independent Mortons of Little London, in whose fleet it was numbered 3111, before returning to Northern Ireland to join Allen's Tours at Belfast. (Autobus Library)

One of several ex-First CentreWest Mercedes-Benz 0530Gs acquired by McGill's, Greenock, J3613 (LK05 FCZ) is seen in Killermont Street, Glasgow, on 26 July 2014 while operating a Commonwealth Games shuttle service. (Murdoch Currie)

Two of Leeds Bradford Airport's three ex-Stagecoach London Mercedes-Benz 0530Gs used on airside duties, BUS 41 and BUS 42 (originally LX04 LBA and LX04 LBE respectively), are seen in their new home in April 2014, still wearing their former owner's livery. (Leeds Bradford International Airport)

One of ten Scania N280UAs purchased new by Menzies in 2010, SA5 (YT10 OBE) is seen here operating a car park shuttle service at London's Heathrow airport. (Author's collection)

Three of First Leeds' Hyperlink-liveried Wright ftr-bodied Volvo B7LAs, headed by 19023 (YJ07 LVR), rest between their duties on the inter-city 72 service in Eastgate, Leeds, on 7 October 2015. (K. A. Jenkinson)

Still in London red livery but with a Red Rocket fleet name on its front panel, independent Catch 22 Bus' ex-Go-Ahead London Central Mercedes-Benz 0530G BL52 ODK is seen here in Blackpool on the express X70 service to Manchester in October 2013. (Alan Robson)

Returned to service to provide transport to the Hospitality Centre at the London Olympic Games in July/August 2012 was Arriva London North Mercedes-Benz 0530G MA11 (BX04 MXJ). (Author's collection)

Liverpool independent Peoplesbus Mercedes-Benz 0530G X1 BUS began life with Go-Ahead London Central, with whom it was registered BX54 UCN. (Author's collection)

Wearing the final style of Travel Coventry livery is National Express West Midlands Mercedes-Benz 0530G 6019 (BJ03 ETF), seen here on 23 April 2010. (R. G. Pope)

Heading through central Birmingham on 15 May 2010, and wearing its final livery, is National Express West Midlands Scania N94UA 6030 (BX54 DNY). (R. G. Pope)

Painted in Unilinx-branded livery for operation on the service to Leicester University's halls of residence is Arriva Midlands Mercedes-Benz 0530G 5000 (BX04 MYG), which had begun life with Arriva London North and is seen here on 4 February 2013. (R. G. Pope)

Seen again, this time after being repainted into its owner's latest livery in 2018, is Arriva Midlands Mercedes-Benz 0530G 5000 (BX04 MYG). (Author's collection)

First Devon & Cornwall Mercedes-Benz 0530G 11037 (SN04 XXY), seen here operating the Eden Project Park & Ride service, was a much-travelled bus, having spent a few weeks operating airside at Leeds Bradford Airport painted in 'Barbie' livery before moving to Devon. Starting life in Dublin with Last Passive, with whom it was registered 04-D-62405, it was later re-registered BN02 EDN before reverting to SN04 XXY. (Author's collection)

Seen on 3 September 2016 while operated by Cyprus International University in Nicosia, and still retaining its London livery, is TNS 118, which began life numbered EA11064 with First CentreWest. (Paul Emery)

Among the numerous ex-London Mercedes-Benz 0530Gs operating in North Cyprus is TPE 653 (originally Go-Ahead London Central MAL83), which is seen here in 2018, owned by Akva, Akcay, and operated on student shuttle services for the European University of Lefke (LAU). (Paul Emery)

Pictured in its new home in North Cyprus in 2018, TPT 215 is one of the Mercedes-Benz 0530Gs purchased by Near East University from Go-Ahead London Central (in whose fleet it was numbered MAL89) for use on student shuttle services. (Paul Emery)

Wearing a colourful 'Happies not Hippies' livery, Brighton & Hove former Go-Ahead London General Mercedes-Benz 0530G 109 (BD57 WDM) is pictured operating the 25 university service in March 2018. (Author's collection)

In the hope of finding buyers, Stagecoach East Scotland school bus-liveried Plaxton-bodied Volvo B10M-55s 51076 (MSU 463, originally P976 UBV), 51098 (CSU 920, originally P198 OSE) and 51099 (127 ASV, originally P199 OSE) stand in the yard of Ensign (dealer), Purfleet, on 27 December 2013. (John Podgorski)

One of two ex-Stagecoach East Scotland Plaxton-bodied Volvo B10M55s transferred from Ensign's dealer stock into its operational fleet, 401 (128 ASV, originally P671 LWB) is seen displaying C2C logos for railway replacement duties on 27 December 2013. (John Podgorski)

Offered for sale or rental by Lombard Finance at the NEC, Birmingham, on 3 October 2013 was former Docklands Buses, London, Mercedes-Benz 0530G 50 (BD52 LNG), which started life numbered MAL50 with Go-Ahead London Central. (K. A. Jenkinson)

Also offered for sale or lease at the National Exhibition Centre, albeit by Dawsonrentals, on 3 October 2013 is ex-First CentreWest Mercedes-Benz 0530G EA11018 (LK53 FBU). (K. A. Jenkinson)

After being taken out of service, one of Manchester Airport's Mercedes-Benz 0530Gs, BU53 ZWV – which had begun life as an EvoBus demonstrator – was 'put out to grass' as a static unit at the airport's Aviation Viewing Park, where it is seen in May 2014. (D. P. B. Davies)

Former Veolia BBA (Holland), Den Oudsten-bodied Volvo YEZ 3559 (originally VJ-34-KB in Holland) is seen here in Belfast acting as an SOS help unit on 25 May 2013. (Paul Savage)

Adorned in East Midlands Airport colours, and seen here operating a Jet Parks shuttle service in March 2018, is Arriva Midlands Mercedes-Benz 0530G 5006 (BX04 NDU), which began life with Arriva London North. (Author's collection)

Seen in the summer of 2018 being used on car park shuttle services at East Midlands Airport is this Arriva Midlands former London Mercedes-Benz 0530G painted in a promotional contravision livery for Jet2 budget airline and displaying registration JET2-2. (Author's collection)

Looking immaculate as it rests between duties at Epsom race course on 5 June 2010 (Derby day) is Go-Ahead London Central Mercedes-Benz 0530G MAL36 (BX04 NBD). (Author's collection)

One of a trio of ex-Brighton & Hove Mercedes-Benz 0530Gs purchased by Leeds Bradford Airport for airside duties, BUS 45 is seen undertaking its duties on 24 June 2017. (K. A. Jenkinson)

Freshly repainted into its owner's new corporate livery, First Aberdeen's ten-year-old Wright-bodied Volvo B7LA 10165 (SV05 DXO) collects its passengers in Union Street, in its home city, on 18 May 2015. (Murdoch Currie)

Opened on 3 September 2018, Belfast Rapid Transit is maintained by a fleet of new Glider-branded Van Hool Exquicity hybrid bendy buses, one of which – 3216 (HGZ 8216) – is seen here on its first day in service. (Paul Savage)

Seen here after being acquired for preservation is Jonckheere-bodied Volvo B10MA-55 51095 (T95 JHN), which began life with Stagecoach Cleveland Transit. (Richard Walter)

Go-South Coast Mercedes-Benz 0530G 4001 (BX02 YYZ), seen here wearing a special livery for operation on the service to Bournemouth University, was new to Go-Ahead London General and has now been preserved. (Author's collection)

After being donated to Alderman Pounder Infant School, Chilwell, by Nottingham City Transport, Wright-bodied Scania L94UA 702 (FP51 EXN) is seen at its new home in 2017. (Author's collection)

Among the newest bendy buses to enter service in the UK are seven Mercedes Benz 0295Gs purchased in June 2017 by OFJ Connections for use at Gatwick airport, where BN17 JOH is seen here. (Author's collection)

In its final resting place at an unknown location, an anonymous ex-London Mercedes-Benz 0530G awaits its ultimate fate. (Author's collection)

Having reached the end of its fourteen-year life, First Manchester Wright-bodied Volvo B10LA 10004 (S995 UJA) awaits its fate in the yard of PVS (breaker), Carlton, on 22 July 2013. Peeping round its front is sister bus 10014 (T515 JNA). (K. A. Jenkinson)

PVS of Carlton's customary method of scrapping bendy buses was to separate the two modules and dismantle them independently. Here, the front and rear sections of a First Manchester Wright-bodied Volvo B10LA stand side by side, awaiting their turn to pass into oblivion on 22 July 2013. (K. A. Jenkinson)

Seen at Floriana, Malta, in April 2014 before making their final journey to the breaker's yard are a number of withdrawn Arriva Malta Mercedes-Benz 0530Gs. (K. S. E. Till)

With vegetation growing around them, a number of former Arriva Malta Mercedes-Benz 530Gs await their fate in a Maltese breaker's yard in November 2015. (K. S. E. Till)

Seen on 19 August 2014, having recently arrived at the overflow premises of Ripley (breaker), Carlton, former Arriva Merseyside's ex-Arriva London North Mercedes-Benz 0530G 6032 (BX04 NDD) will soon be removed onwards to the main yard, where it will be converted into a pile of twisted metal. (K. A. Jenkinson)

Pictured in pouring rain while stored in the spring of 2017 at bus operator Connexions, Rufforth, by Ripley (breaker), is ex-Stagecoach East London 23041 (LX04 KZN), which would ultimately be removed to its owner's Carlton yard for dismantling. (Author's collection)

Having remained in store since being withdrawn by First Leeds in 2014, Wright ftr-bodied Volvo B7LA 19014 (YJ56 EAA) was sold during the spring of 2018 to PVS (breakers), Carlton, where it is seen on 26 September awaiting its fate. (K. A. Jenkinson)

Pictured at PVS of Carlton's yard on 26 September 2018, National Express Coventry Mercedes-Benz 0530G 6020 (BJ03 ETK), which was seen earlier in the book while still in service, may possibly have a future as it was marked 'Do not touch', whereas the five First Leeds Wright FTR-bodied Volvo B7LAs will not be as fortunate and are all awaiting scrapping. (K. A. Jenkinson)